PASTA
SAUCES

60 easy recipes
for making good food fast

HAMLYN

First published in Great Britain in 1994 by
Hamlyn, an imprint of Reed Consumer Books Limited
Michelin House, 81 Fulham Road, London SW3 6RB
and Auckland, Melbourne, Singapore and Toronto

Copyright © 1994 Reed International Books Limited

ISBN 0-600-58256-6

A CIP catalogue record for this book
is available from the British Library

ACKNOWLEDGEMENTS
Designed and produced by: The Bridgewater Book Company
Series Editors: Veronica Sperling and Christine McFadden
Art Director: Peter Bridgewater
Designer: Terry Jeavons
Photography: Trevor Wood
Food preparation and styling: Jonathan Higgins
Cookery contributor: Christine McFadden

Produced by Mandarin Offset
Printed and bound in Singapore

NOTES

- Standard level spoon measurements are used in all recipes.
- Both imperial and metric measurements have been given in all recipes. Use one set of measurements only and not a mixture of both.
- Eggs should be size 3 unless otherwise stated.
- Milk should be full fat unless otherwise stated.
- Fresh herbs should be used unless otherwise stated. If unavailable use dried herbs as an alternative but halve the quantites stated.
- Ovens should be preheated to the specified temperature - if using a fan assisted oven, follow manufacturer's instructions for adjusting the time and the temperature.
- All microwave information is based on a 650 watt oven. Follow manufacturer's instructions for an oven with a different wattage.

Contents

Introduction
4 ~ 5

❦

Meat and Poultry Sauces
6 ~ 25

❦

Vegetable Sauces
26 ~ 47

❦

Fish Sauces
48 ~ 63

❦

Index
64

Introduction

$\mathcal{C}$OOKED in a matter of minutes, pasta is one of the most versatile and comforting of foods, combining happily with an endless variety of sauces.

Types of Pasta

There are two basic types of pasta: dried flour-and-water pasta made with hard durum wheat flour (semolina), and egg pasta made with plain flour and eggs. Egg pasta may be dried or fresh, and flavoured with spinach, tomato, mushroom or cuttlefish ink. There are also various Asian noodles, made from rice flour, mung beans or buckwheat.

Shop-bought dried pasta is often a better choice than shop-bought fresh pasta, which can sometimes be thick and rubbery. Dried pasta goes well with robust oil-based sauces. Fresh pasta is more absorbent than dried pasta, and goes well with delicate butter- or cream-enriched sauces.

Pasta Shapes

Pasta is made in an extraordinary number of shapes, each lending itself to a particular type of sauce. For instance, long round pasta is best for tomato- or oil-based sauces which will cling to the pasta. Egg pasta ribbons go well with butter- or cream-based sauces. Tubes and shapes are ideal for trapping chunkier sauces in their crevices.

LONG ROUND PASTA: Spaghetti, capelli d'angelo, vermicelli, bucatini, fusilli lunghi.
RIBBONS: Tagliatelle, pappardelle, linguine, fettuccine, taglioline, lasagnette.
TUBES: Penne, rigatoni, macaroni.
SHAPES: Fusilli, farfalle, lumache, conchiglie, gnocchi, orecchiette.

Cooking Perfect Pasta

Always cook the sauce before the pasta. The sauce can usually be kept waiting, but if you leave cooked pasta to stand, it will start to become sticky.

It is hard to specify an exact serving size but as a rough guide, 450 g/1 lb of pasta serves 4–6 as a main course. If a greater ratio of sauce to pasta is needed, or the dish is very rich, 350 g/12 oz of pasta is enough.

Use a very large pan. You will need 1 litre/$1\frac{3}{4}$ pints of water and 1 teaspoon of salt for every 100 g/4 oz of pasta.

Bring the water to a fast boil, then add the salt and pasta, stirring to prevent sticking. There is no need to add olive oil if you use the correct amount of water. Cover the pan until the water boils again, then remove the lid.

The cooking time depends on the pasta. Freshly made egg pasta cooks in less than a minute, but shop-bought dried pasta can take up to 15 minutes. The only way is to test periodically for 'doneness'. The pasta should be 'al dente' – firm to bite and chewy. Do not over-cook it, otherwise you will end up with a sticky mess.

Drain the pasta as soon as it is 'al dente', without rinsing. Transfer it to a warm serving bowl, or return it to the hot pan. Toss the pasta with the sauce until heated through.

FROM LEFT, TOP TO BOTTOM
Row 1: black tagliatelle, tomato taglioline, egg taglioline
Row 2: tagliatelle, black spaghetti, spinach tagliatelle
Row 3: spaghetti
Row 4: spinach spaghetti
Row 5: orecchiette, fusilli bucati, macaroni, farfalle
Row 6: gnocchi, conchiglie, penne, fusilli

Prosciutto and Pea Sauce

SERVES 4-6

50 g/2 oz butter
225 g/8 oz prosciutto, diced
300 g/10 oz frozen petit pois, thawed
6 spring onions, green parts included, finely sliced

300 ml/½ pint whipping cream
salt and freshly ground black pepper
50 g/2 oz freshly grated Parmesan cheese
450 g/1 lb conchiglie or gnocchi

*M*ELT the butter in a pan, add the prosciutto, and gently fry for 1–2 minutes until lightly browned.

❧ Add the peas and spring onions, and fry for 2–3 minutes.

❧ Pour in the cream, and season lightly with salt and pepper. Simmer over a medium-high heat, stirring constantly, until thickened. Stir in the Parmesan cheese.

❧ Cook the pasta in boiling salted water until 'al dente'. Drain and toss with the sauce. Serve immediately.

Bolognese Sauce

SERVES 4-6

3 tbsp olive oil
25 g/1 oz butter
½ small onion, finely chopped
½ small carrot, finely chopped
1 small celery stalk, diced
25 g/1 oz mushrooms, diced
1 garlic clove, finely chopped
50 g/2 oz ham or lean bacon, diced
350 g/12 oz lean minced beef
125 ml/4 fl oz dry red wine

2 tbsp finely chopped fresh parsley
salt and freshly ground black pepper
2 tsp plain flour
4 tbsp tomato purée
300 ml/½ pint stock
150 ml/¼ pint double cream
450 g/1 lb fettuccine or spaghetti
chopped fresh parsley, to garnish
freshly grated Parmesan cheese, to serve

*H*EAT the oil and butter in a pan, and add the onion, carrot, celery, mushrooms and garlic. Gently fry until lightly browned. Add the ham and beef and fry until the beef is browned. Add the wine and parsley, and season to taste.

❧ When the wine has reduced, stir in the flour. Simmer very gently for 10–15 minutes, stirring constantly.

❧ Add the tomato purée and a little of the stock. Simmer gently, covered, for 1½ hours, gradually stirring in the remaining stock. Stir in the cream and simmer, uncovered, until reduced.

❧ Cook the pasta in boiling salted water until 'al dente'. Drain and toss with half the sauce. Transfer to a serving dish and spoon the remaining sauce over the top. Garnish with parsley, and serve immediately with Parmesan cheese.

Sausage and Tomato Sauce

SERVES 4

1 tbsp olive oil
1 large onion, chopped
2 garlic cloves, crushed
450 g/1 lb Italian sausage, peeled and roughly chopped
1 red pepper, seeded and cut into 1 cm/½ inch squares

700 g/1½ lb tomatoes, peeled and chopped
2 tsp dried oregano
2 tbsp tomato purée
salt and freshly ground black pepper
225 g/8 oz macaroni or rigatoni
25 g/1 oz butter

*H*EAT the oil in a pan, and gently fry the onion until soft. Add the garlic, and fry until beginning to colour.

❧ Add the sausage to the pan and fry until evenly browned.

❧ Add the red pepper, tomatoes, oregano and tomato purée, and season to taste with salt and pepper. Cook gently, uncovered, for 12–15 minutes.

❧ Cook the pasta in boiling salted water until 'al dente'. Drain well and stir in the butter.

❧ Toss the pasta with the sauce and transfer to a warm serving dish. Serve immediately.

Ham and Mushroom Sauce

SERVES 3-4

25 g/1 oz butter
100 g/4 oz mushrooms, sliced
175 g/6 oz cooked ham, cut into matchstick strips
225 g/8 oz conchiglie or gnocchi
150 ml/¼ pint double cream

175 g/6 oz Cheddar cheese, grated
salt and freshly ground black pepper
1 tbsp finely chopped fresh parsley
pitted black olives, to garnish
2 tbsp freshly grated Parmesan cheese, to garnish

*M*ELT the butter in a pan. Add the mushrooms and ham, and fry for about 5 minutes until softened.

❧ Cook the pasta in boiling, salted water until 'al dente'. Drain thoroughly. Toss with the mushroom mixture.

❧ Mix together the cream and cheese, and season to taste with salt and pepper. Stir the cream mixture and parsley into the pasta, and toss quickly over a very low heat until well coated and slightly thickened.

❧ Transfer to a serving dish. Garnish with olives and sprinkle with the Parmesan cheese. Serve immediately.

Chinese Chicken and Mushroom Sauce

SERVES 4

8 Chinese dried mushrooms or
   225 g/8 oz fresh shitake mushrooms
200 g/7 oz boneless, skinless chicken
   breasts cut into matchstick strips
2 tsp cornflour
8 tbsp soy sauce
4 tbsp sherry
2 tsp salt
2 tsp sugar

300 g/11 oz egg noodles
1 litre/1¾ pints chicken stock
8 tbsp vegetable oil
225 g/8 oz bamboo shoots, cut into
   matchstick strips
225 g/8 oz spinach, finely sliced
4 spring onions, finely chopped
2 slices fresh ginger root, finely
   chopped

$\mathscr{S}$OAK the Chinese dried mushrooms, if using, in warm water for about 20 minutes. Squeeze out the moisture, and discard the hard stalks. Cut the mushrooms into thin shreds.

❧ Mix the chicken with the cornflour. Combine the soy sauce, sherry, salt and sugar.

❧ Bring a saucepan of water to the boil, add the noodles and simmer for 5 minutes until soft but not sticky. Drain and place in a heated serving dish.

❧ Bring the stock to the boil and pour over the cooked noodles.

❧ Heat the oil in a wok, and stir-fry the chicken, bamboo shoots, mushrooms, spinach, spring onions and ginger for 1 minute.

❧ Add the soy sauce mixture and stir-fry for 2 minutes. Toss with the noodles, and serve immediately.

Chicken and Tomato Sauce

SERVES 4-6

2 tbsp olive oil
225 g/8 oz boneless, skinless chicken
   breasts, diced
1 large onion, finely chopped
3 celery stalks, diced
2 carrots, diced

2 tsp dried oregano
125 ml/4 fl oz red wine
400 g/14 oz can chopped tomatoes
salt and freshly ground black pepper
350 g/12 oz conchiglie, gnocchi or
   penne

$\mathscr{H}$EAT the oil in a pan, and fry the chicken, stirring occasionally, until lightly coloured. Add the onion, celery and carrots, and cook for 5 minutes until softened.

❧ Add the oregano, wine and tomatoes, and season to taste. Bring to the boil, cover and simmer for 10 minutes.

❧ Cook the pasta in boiling salted water until 'al dente'. Drain and toss with half the sauce. Transfer to a serving dish, spoon the remaining sauce over the top and serve immediately.

Pork Chow Mein

SERVES 6

450 g/1 lb egg noodles
275 g/10 oz pork fillet, cut into
   matchstick strips
3 tsp cornflour
2 tbsp soy sauce
1 tbsp dry sherry
1 tsp salt
1 tsp sugar

5 tbsp groundnut oil
100 g/4 oz bamboo shoots, cut into
   matchstick strips
½ cucumber, cut into matchstick
   strips
100 g/4 oz spinach, shredded
1 tsp dark sesame oil

*B*RING a saucepan of water to the boil, add the noodles and simmer for 5 minutes until soft but not sticky. Drain thoroughly and rinse with cold water.

❦ Mix the pork with 2 teaspoons of the cornflour. Mix together the soy sauce, sherry, salt, sugar and remaining cornflour.

❦ Heat half the groundnut oil in a wok. Place the noodles in a large bowl, separating them with a fork. Pour over the hot oil, stirring to coat. Return the noodles to the wok, stir-fry for 2–3 minutes, then place on a serving dish.

❦ Heat the remaining groundnut oil, and stir-fry the bamboo shoots, cucumber, spinach and pork for 3 minutes.

❦ Add the soy sauce mixture, and stir until thickened. Pour the mixture over the noodles, sprinkle with the sesame oil and serve immediately.

Chicken Liver Sauce

SERVES 4

2 tbsp oil
½ onion, finely chopped
1 garlic clove, finely chopped
350 g/12 oz chicken livers, chopped
1 tbsp finely chopped fresh parsley
1 tbsp finely chopped fresh marjoram

175 g/6 oz mushrooms, sliced
150 ml/¼ pint red wine
150 ml/¼ pint stock
salt and freshly ground black pepper
350 g/12 oz tagliatelle, lasagnette or
   pappardelle

*H*EAT the oil, and fry the onion and garlic for 5 minutes until soft. Add the livers, herbs and mushrooms, and fry until the livers are lightly browned.

❦ Add the wine and stock, and season well. Bring to the boil, stirring, then cover and simmer for 15 minutes.

❦ Cook the pasta in boiling salted water until 'al dente'. Drain and toss with half the sauce. Transfer to a serving dish and spoon the remaining sauce over the top. Serve immediately.

Spinach Tagliatelle with Bacon and Fennel

SERVES 4-6

6 rashers unsmoked streaky bacon
2 tbsp olive oil
2 fennel bulbs, chopped
2 garlic cloves, finely chopped
4 tbsp freshly grated Parmesan cheese

300 ml/½ pint fromage frais
3 tbsp finely chopped fresh parsley
salt and freshly ground black pepper
350 g/12 oz spinach tagliatelle
fennel fronds, to garnish

GRILL the bacon until crisp. Drain on paper towels and set aside.

❧ Heat the oil in a pan and add the fennel and garlic. Cover and cook over a low heat for 5 minutes until the fennel is just tender.

❧ Add the Parmesan cheese, fromage frais and parsley, and season to taste. Simmer over a low heat for 1–2 minutes.

❧ Cook the pasta in boiling salted water until 'al dente'. Drain and toss with the sauce. Transfer to a heated serving dish.

❧ Chop the bacon and sprinkle over the pasta. Garnish with fennel fronds and serve at once.

Ham, Tomato and Cheese Sauce

SERVES 6

40 g/1½ oz butter
1 tbsp olive oil
3 garlic cloves, finely chopped
175 g/6 oz cooked ham, finely diced
400 g/14 oz can chopped tomatoes

salt and freshly ground black pepper
450 g/1 lb macaroni
2 tbsp chopped fresh basil
100 g/4 oz freshly grated pecorino or Parmesan cheese

HEAT the butter and oil over a medium heat. Add the garlic and ham, and gently fry for 4–5 minutes. Add the tomatoes, and salt and pepper to taste. Simmer for 10–15 minutes, or until well blended, stirring frequently.

❧ Cook the macaroni in boiling salted water until 'al dente'. Drain and toss with half the sauce. Transfer to a serving dish and spoon the remaining sauce over the top.

❧ Mix the basil with the cheese and sprinkle over the macaroni. Serve immediately.

Pork and Rosemary Sauce

SERVES 4-6

3 tbsp olive oil
½ onion, finely chopped
1 carrot, finely diced
2 celery stalks, finely diced
2 garlic cloves, finely chopped
450 g/1 lb pork fillet, cut into
   1 cm/½ inch cubes
2 tsp finely chopped fresh rosemary
finely grated zest of ½ lemon

salt and freshly ground black pepper
400 g/14 oz can chopped tomatoes
225 ml/8 fl oz stock
450 g/1 lb conchiglie or gnocchi
50 g/2 oz freshly grated Parmesan
   cheese
25 g/1 oz butter
2 tbsp chopped fresh flat-leafed
   parsley, to garnish

HEAT the oil in a saucepan and gently fry the onion until golden. Add the carrot, celery and garlic, and gently fry for about 5 minutes.

❦ Stir in the pork, rosemary and lemon zest, and fry until the pork is lightly browned. Season to taste.

❦ Add the tomatoes and stock. Bring to the boil, then simmer over a low heat for 30 minutes.

❦ Cook the pasta in boiling salted water until 'al dente'. Drain and toss with the Parmesan cheese, butter and half the sauce.

❦ Transfer to a serving dish, and spoon the remaining sauce over the top. Garnish with the parsley and serve immediately.

Pancetta with Flageolet Beans, Garlic and Chilli

SERVES 4-6

2 tbsp olive oil
250 g/9 oz pancetta or smoked streaky
   bacon, diced
2 garlic cloves, finely chopped
½ tsp dried chilli flakes

400 g/14 oz can flageolet beans,
   drained and rinsed
300 ml/½ pint whipping cream
salt and freshly ground black pepper
450 g/1 lb penne or fusilli
2 tbsp chopped fresh coriander

HEAT the oil, and fry the pancetta until lightly browned. Add the garlic and chilli flakes, and fry until the garlic is just pale golden.

❦ Gently stir in the beans, cream, and salt and pepper. Simmer for a few minutes until heated through.

❦ Cook the pasta in boiling salted water until 'al dente'. Drain and toss with half the sauce.

❦ Transfer to a serving dish and spoon the remaining sauce over the top. Sprinkle with the coriander and serve immediately.

Pancetta and Celery Sauce

SERVES 4-6

75 g/3 oz butter
225 g/8 oz pancetta, diced
1 carrot, diced
4 celery stalks, diced
1 garlic clove, finely chopped

3 tbsp tomato purée
225 ml/8 fl oz chicken stock
salt and freshly ground black pepper
450 g/1 lb penne or rigatoni
freshly grated Parmesan cheese

*M*ELT 50 g/2 oz of the butter in a saucepan. Add the pancetta, carrot, celery and garlic, and gently fry for 5 minutes.

❧ Stir in the tomato purée and stock, and season to taste. Bring to the boil and simmer for 15 minutes.

❧ Cook the pasta in boiling salted water until 'al dente'. Drain and toss with the remaining butter and half the sauce. Transfer to a serving dish and spoon the remaining sauce over the top. Sprinkle with Parmesan cheese and serve immediately.

Rabbit and Red Wine Sauce

SERVES 4-6

500 g/18 oz rabbit or skinless chicken, jointed
2 tbsp olive oil
1 onion, chopped
1 celery stalk, chopped
1 carrot, diced
100 g/4 oz pancetta or bacon, diced
2 garlic cloves, crushed
1 tbsp flour
1 tbsp tomato purée

150 ml/¼ pint red wine
150 ml/¼ pint stock
400 g/14 oz can chopped tomatoes
1 tbsp chopped fresh parsley
½ tsp dried oregano
pinch of nutmeg
salt and freshly ground black pepper
450 g/1 lb tagliatelle or pappardelle
50 g/2 oz freshly grated Parmesan cheese

*C*UT all the meat off the bones, and chop fairly finely. Heat the oil in a pan, and fry the onion, celery, carrot and bacon for 6–7 minutes.

❧ Add the meat, garlic, flour and tomato purée. Gently fry for 15 minutes, then add the wine. Simmer for a few minutes, then add the stock, tomatoes, herbs and nutmeg, and season to taste. Simmer gently for 1 hour or until the meat is tender and the mixture fairly thick.

❧ Cook the pasta in boiling salted water until 'al dente'. Drain, stir in the Parmesan cheese and toss with half the sauce. Transfer to a serving dish, and spoon the remaining sauce over the top. Serve immediately.

Ham, Pea and Mushroom Sauce

SERVES 4-6

50 g/2 oz butter
225 g/8 oz mushrooms, thinly sliced
salt and freshly ground black pepper
100 g/4 oz frozen peas
300 ml/½ pint single cream

100 g/4 oz lean cooked ham, cut into
   matchstick strips
100 g/4 oz freshly grated Parmesan
   cheese
450 g/1 lb tagliatelle or fettuccine

*M*ELT half the butter, and gently fry the mushrooms until just tender. Season to taste with salt and pepper.
❦ Cook the peas in boiling salted water and drain.
❦ Put the remaining butter and the cream into a saucepan, and heat gently without allowing the mixture to boil.
❦ Add the mushrooms with their juice, the peas and the ham. Add one-third of the Parmesan cheese.
❦ Cook the pasta in boiling salted water until 'al dente'. Drain and toss with half the sauce. Transfer to a serving dish and spoon the remaining sauce over the top. Serve immediately with the remaining Parmesan cheese.

Spaghetti alla Carbonara
(Bacon and Egg Sauce)

SERVES 4-6

3 tbsp olive oil
1 garlic clove, lightly crushed
225 g/8 oz streaky bacon chopped
3 tbsp dry white wine
3 eggs

75 g/3 oz freshly grated Parmesan
   cheese
3 tbsp finely chopped fresh parsley
salt and freshly ground black pepper
350 g/12 oz spaghetti

*H*EAT the oil in a pan, and gently fry the garlic until golden. Remove from the pan. Add the bacon and fry for 2 minutes over a fairly high heat until crisp.
❦ Add the wine, and simmer until it has evaporated.
❦ Beat together the eggs, Parmesan cheese, parsley, and salt and pepper to taste.
❦ Cook the spaghetti in a large pan of boiling salted water until 'al dente'. Drain thoroughly and return to the pan.
❦ Immediately stir in the beaten egg mixture and the bacon, and continue stirring until the heat from the spaghetti cooks the eggs. Transfer to a serving dish and serve at once.

Bacon, Mushroom and Tomato Sauce

SERVES 4-6

100 g/4 oz butter
175 g/6 oz lean bacon, diced
350 g/12 oz mushrooms, sliced
2 garlic cloves, sliced
½ fresh chilli
450 g/1 lb tomatoes, peeled and
  chopped

fresh basil leaves, torn
salt
450 g/1 lb penne or macaroni
100 g/4 oz freshly grated Parmesan or
  pecorino cheese

*M*ELT half the butter in a frying pan, add the bacon and gently fry until lightly browned. Remove from the pan with a slotted spoon, and drain on paper towels.

❧ Fry the mushrooms in the butter remaining in the pan. Remove with a slotted spoon, and set aside.

❧ Fry the garlic and the chilli in the same pan. When the garlic is golden brown, discard it together with the chilli.

❧ Add the tomatoes to the pan with the basil. Season with salt and simmer for 20 minutes.

❧ Stir in the bacon and mushrooms, and simmer gently for a few minutes.

❧ Cook the pasta in boiling salted water until 'al dente'. Drain and transfer to a heated serving dish. Toss with the cheese and the remaining butter. Pour the sauce over the top, toss gently and serve immediately.

Prosciutto, Chilli and Tomato Sauce

SERVES 4-6

4 tbsp olive oil
1 onion, finely chopped
100 g/4 oz prosciutto, diced
2 garlic cloves, crushed
1 fresh chilli, seeded and finely
  chopped

700 g/1½ lb tomatoes, peeled and
  chopped
salt and freshly ground black pepper
450 g/1 lb fettuccine or tagliatelle
75 g/3 oz freshly grated pecorino
  cheese

*H*EAT the oil in a pan, and gently fry the onion for 3 minutes. Add the prosciutto and cook for a further 2–3 minutes. Add the garlic, chilli and tomatoes, and season to taste. Cook gently for 10 minutes until thickened.

❧ Cook the pasta in boiling salted water until 'al dente'. Drain and toss with the sauce and grated pecorino. Transfer to a heated serving dish and serve immediately.

Bacon and Broad Bean Sauce

SERVES 4-6

350 g/12 oz small shelled broad beans
25 g/1 oz butter
2 shallots, finely chopped
225 g/8 oz unsmoked streaky bacon, diced
2 tsp chopped fresh thyme
grated zest of ½ lemon

300 ml/½ pint whipping cream
freshly ground black pepper
450 g/1 lb gnocchi or conchiglie
3 tbsp chopped fresh flat-leafed parsley
freshly grated Parmesan cheese, to serve

*P*LUNGE the broad beans into boiling water for 2 minutes. Drain under cold running water, then slip off the outer skins if they are tough.

❧ Melt the butter, and gently fry the shallots and bacon for 4–5 minutes.

❧ Stir in the thyme, lemon zest, cream, and pepper. Bring to the boil and simmer for 5 minutes. Stir in the broad beans.

❧ Cook the pasta in boiling salted water until 'al dente'. Drain and toss with half the sauce and the parsley. Transfer to a serving dish, spoon the remaining sauce over the top, and serve immediately with Parmesan cheese.

Conchiglie with Peperoni, Onion and Balsamic Vinegar

SERVES 4-6

5 tbsp olive oil
3 large onions, thinly sliced into rings
250 g/9 oz peperoni, sliced
300 ml/½ pint stock

4 tbsp chopped fresh flat-leafed parsley
1 tbsp balsamic vinegar
salt and freshly ground black pepper
350 g/12 oz conchiglie or gnocchi

*H*EAT the oil in a large pan, and fry the onions over a low heat for 40 minutes, until very soft and slightly caramelized.

❧ Raise the heat, add the peperoni and stir-fry for a few minutes until heated through.

❧ Pour in the stock and bring to the boil, scraping up any sediment from the bottom of the pan.

❧ Stir in the parsley and vinegar, and season to taste.

❧ Cook the pasta in boiling salted water until 'al dente'. Drain, toss with the sauce and serve immediately.

Avocado and Cream Sauce

SERVES 6-8

350 g/12 oz conchiglie or fusilli
1 ripe avocado, halved and stoned
juice of 1 lemon
1 garlic clove, crushed
1 tsp caster sugar

150 ml/¼ pint single cream
salt and freshly ground black pepper
4 spring onions, chopped
2 tbsp chopped fresh parsley

*C*ook the pasta in boiling salted water until 'al dente'.
Drain and cool.

❧ Scoop the avocado flesh out of the skin and place in a blender
or food processor with the lemon juice, garlic, sugar and cream.
Purée until smooth. Season to taste with salt and pepper.

❧ Add the sauce to the pasta with the spring onions and
parsley. Toss well together. Serve lightly chilled.

Raw Tomato Sauce with Basil

SERVES 4

450 g/1 lb ripe plum tomatoes, peeled
3 tbsp olive oil
1 garlic clove, crushed
bunch of fresh basil

salt
350 g/12 oz penne, conchiglie or
farfalle

*P*urée the tomatoes briefly in a blender. Add the oil and
crushed garlic.

❧ Wash and dry the basil leaves, discarding the stalks. Tear the
leaves into small pieces, and add to the sauce.

❧ Leave the sauce to stand for about 30 minutes. Add salt to
taste, and stir well.

❧ Cook the pasta in boiling salted water until 'al dente'. Drain
and transfer to a serving dish. Pour the sauce over the top and
serve immediately.

Chick-Pea and Tomato Sauce

SERVES 4-6

400 g/14 oz can chick-peas, rinsed and drained
6 tbsp olive oil
1 small onion, finely chopped
1 celery stalk, diced
2 garlic cloves, finely chopped
1½ x 400 g/14 oz cans chopped tomatoes

2 tbsp chopped fresh flat-leafed parsley
1 tsp finely chopped fresh rosemary
salt and freshly ground black pepper
350 g/12 oz tagliatelle or pappardelle
4 tbsp freshly grated Parmesan cheese

*P*URÉE half the chick-peas in a blender, adding a little water if necessary.

🌢 Heat the oil and gently fry the onion and celery until just soft. Add the garlic and fry until just beginning to colour.

🌢 Add the tomatoes, parsley, rosemary, and salt and pepper.

🌢 Simmer for 10–15 minutes until thickened. Stir in the puréed and whole chick-peas, and simmer for another 5 minutes.

🌢 Cook the pasta in boiling salted water until 'al dente'. Drain and toss with half the sauce. Stir in half the Parmesan cheese.

🌢 Transfer to a serving dish and spoon the remaining sauce over the top. Dust with the remaining Parmesan cheese and serve at once.

Rocket, Garlic and Chilli Sauce

SERVES 4

350 g/12 oz wholewheat fusilli
8 tbsp olive oil
3 garlic cloves, finely chopped
¼ tsp dried chilli flakes

100 g/4 oz rocket, roughly chopped
salt and freshly ground black pepper
50 g/2 oz freshly grated Parmesan cheese

*C*OOK the pasta in boiling salted water until 'al dente'. Meanwhile, heat the oil and gently fry the garlic and chilli flakes until the garlic begins to colour.

🌢 Add the rocket and stir until just wilted. Season to taste.

🌢 Drain the pasta and toss with the sauce and Parmesan cheese. Serve at once.

Aubergine, Pepper and Olive Sauce

SERVES 4-6

4 tbsp olive oil
1 onion, finely chopped
400 g/14 oz can chopped tomatoes
2 tbsp tomato purée
150 ml/¼ pint red wine
1 large aubergine, chopped
1 large red pepper, seeded and finely diced

1 large green pepper, seeded and finely diced
8 anchovy fillets, drained and chopped
1 garlic clove, crushed
450 g/1 lb spaghetti or linguine
75 g/3 oz pitted black olives
salt and freshly ground black pepper

*H*EAT the oil in a pan, and gently fry the onion for 3 minutes. Add the tomatoes, tomato purée, red wine, aubergine, peppers, anchovy fillets and garlic. Simmer gently for 20 minutes.

❧ Cook the pasta in boiling salted water until 'al dente'. Drain and toss with the sauce, adding the olives, and salt and pepper to taste. Serve immediately.

Fresh Herb and Lemon Sauce

SERVES 4-6

350 g/12 oz farfalle or fusilli
10 tbsp olive oil
8 spring onions, green parts included, finely chopped
finely grated zest of 1 lemon

75 g/3 oz trimmed mixed fresh herbs (flat-leafed parsley, rocket, thyme, marjoram, basil, rosemary), chopped
4 tbsp toasted breadcrumbs
50 g/2 oz freshly grated Parmesan cheese
salt and freshly ground black pepper

*C*OOK the pasta in boiling salted water until 'al dente'. Drain and transfer to a heated serving dish.

❧ Heat the oil until very hot. Remove from the heat and immediately stir in the spring onions, lemon zest and herbs.

❧ Toss with the pasta, breadcrumbs and Parmesan cheese, and season generously with salt and pepper. Serve immediately.

Leek and Green Peppercorn Sauce

SERVES 4-6

3 tbsp olive oil
700 g/1½ lb leeks, sliced lengthways
 and cut into matchstick strips
2 tsp green peppercorns, crushed
3 tbsp chopped fresh flat-leafed parsley

300 ml/½ pint whipping cream
salt
450 g/1 lb tagliatelle or fettuccine
4 tbsp freshly grated Parmesan
 cheese

*H*EAT the oil in a pan and gently fry the leeks with the green peppercorns for 3–4 minutes until the leeks are just tender. Stir in the parsley and cream, and season to taste.
❦ Cook the pasta in boiling salted water until 'al dente'. Drain and toss with the sauce. Stir in the Parmesan cheese and serve at once.

Pesto Sauce

SERVES 4

2 garlic cloves, crushed
50 g/2 oz fresh basil leaves
2 tbsp pine nuts
8 tbsp olive oil
50 g/2 oz freshly grated Parmesan
 cheese
2 tbsp freshly grated pecorino Romano
 cheese

salt and freshly ground black pepper
450 g/1 lb spaghetti or linguine
knob of butter
freshly grated Parmesan or pecorino
 Romano cheese, to serve

*P*URÉE the garlic, basil, pine nuts and olive oil in a blender or food processor until smooth.
❦ Transfer to a bowl and stir in the cheeses. Season with salt and pepper to taste.
❦ Cook the pasta in boiling salted water until 'al dente'. Drain and transfer to a warm serving dish.
❦ Toss with the sauce and top with the knob of butter. Serve with the additional Parmesan or pecorino cheese.

Cream Cheese and Walnut Sauce

SERVES 4-6

25 g/1 oz butter
350 g/12 oz mascarpone or full-fat cream cheese
50 g/2 oz freshly grated Parmesan cheese

100 g/4 oz shelled walnuts, coarsely chopped
1 tbsp snipped fresh chives
salt and freshly ground black pepper
450 g/1 lb farfalle or conchiglie

*M*ELT the butter in a pan, add the cream cheese and heat very gently, without boiling, until melted.
❦ Add the Parmesan cheese, walnuts and chives and heat through. Season to taste with salt and pepper.
❦ Cook the pasta in boiling salted water until 'al dente'. Drain and toss with the sauce. Transfer to a serving dish, and serve immediately.

Tomato, Anchovy and Olive Sauce

SERVES 4-6

5 tbsp olive oil
25 g/1 oz butter
3 garlic cloves, finely chopped
1–2 fresh chillies, seeded and finely chopped
75 g/3 oz anchovy fillets, drained and chopped
175 g/6 oz oil-cured black olives, pitted and roughly chopped

1½ tbsp capers, drained
700 g/1½ lb tomatoes, peeled and chopped
2 tbsp tomato purée
salt and freshly ground black pepper
1 tbsp chopped fresh basil
3 tbsp chopped fresh flat-leafed parsley
450 g/1 lb spaghetti or linguine

*H*EAT the oil and butter in a pan, and gently fry the garlic, chilli and anchovies, until the garlic begins to change colour.
❦ Add the olives, capers, tomatoes and tomato purée. Simmer over a very low heat for 30 minutes until thickened.
❦ Season with salt only if necessary, and a little pepper.
❦ Add the basil and half the parsley.
❦ Cook the pasta in boiling salted water until 'al dente'. Drain and toss with half the sauce. Transfer to a serving dish and spoon the remaining sauce over the top. Sprinkle with the remaining parsley and serve immediately.

Aubergine, Tomato and Chilli Sauce

SERVES 4-6

8 tbsp olive oil
1 large aubergine, cut into 1 cm/
  ½ inch cubes
2 garlic cloves, finely chopped
1 fresh chilli, seeded and finely
  chopped

2 x 400 g/14 oz cans chopped
  tomatoes
salt and freshly ground black pepper
3 tbsp chopped fresh flat-leafed
  parsley
450 g/1 lb fusilli lunghi or fettuccine
freshly grated Parmesan cheese

*H*EAT the oil in a large pan and gently fry the aubergine for about 5 minutes. Stir in the garlic and chilli, and fry until the garlic begins to colour.

❦ Stir in the tomatoes, salt and pepper, and parsley. Simmer for about 30 minutes.

❦ Cook the pasta in boiling salted water until 'al dente'. Drain and toss with half the sauce. Transfer to a serving dish, and spoon the remaining sauce over the top. Dust with Parmesan cheese and serve at once.

Farfalle with Herbed Savoy Cabbage

SERVES 4-6

8 tbsp olive oil
2 garlic cloves, finely chopped
800 g/1¾ lb Savoy cabbage, shredded
salt and freshly ground black pepper
finely grated zest of 1 lemon
3 tbsp chopped fresh flat-leafed
  parsley

1 tbsp chopped fresh dill
1 tbsp chopped fresh mint
25 g/1 oz butter
450 g/1 lb farfalle or fusilli
4 tbsp freshly grated Parmesan cheese

*H*EAT the olive oil in a large frying pan. Add the garlic and cabbage, and gently fry for 2 minutes, tossing the leaves to coat them with oil.

❦ Season to taste, then cover and cook over a medium heat for 10 minutes, until the cabbage is tender but still crisp. Add a little water if necessary, to prevent sticking.

❦ Uncover the pan and raise the heat. Stir in the lemon zest, herbs and butter.

❦ Cook the pasta in boiling salted water until 'al dente'. Drain and toss with the cabbage. Stir in the Parmesan cheese and serve at once.

Broccoli Sauce with Chilli

SERVES 4-6

450 g/1 lb broccoli florets
450 g/1 lb fusilli, orecchiette or
   conchiglie
salt and freshly ground black pepper

dried chilli flakes, to taste
50 g/2 oz butter
100 g/4 oz freshly grated Parmesan
   cheese

*C*ook the broccoli florets in lightly salted boiling water for 3 minutes until just tender. Drain and break into smaller pieces. Dice the stalks.

❦ Cook the pasta in boiling salted water until 'al dente'. Drain and transfer to a warm serving dish, reserving a little of the pasta water.

❦ Add the broccoli, salt and pepper, chilli flakes, butter and half the Parmesan cheese. Mix well, adding a little pasta water if necessary to keep the mixture moist.

❦ Serve with the remaining Parmesan cheese.

Roasted Peppers with Coriander and Chilli Pesto

SERVES 6

3 mixed red and yellow peppers
50 g/2 oz trimmed fresh coriander,
   roughly chopped
1 fresh chilli, seeded and roughly
   chopped
2 garlic cloves, crushed
2 tbsp pine nuts

finely grated zest of 1 lime
1 tsp salt
8 tbsp olive oil
50 g/2 oz freshly grated Parmesan
   cheese
450 g/1 lb spaghetti or fettuccine
50 g/2 oz butter, diced

*R*oast the peppers in a preheated oven at 220°C/425°F/ gas mark 7, until the skins blacken on all sides.

❦ Remove the skins and seeds, then chop the flesh into 1 cm/ ½ inch dice.

❦ Put the coriander and chillies in a blender or food processor with the garlic, pine nuts, lime zest and salt. Purée until smooth, gradually adding the olive oil. Transfer to a bowl and mix with the Parmesan cheese.

❦ Cook the pasta in boiling salted water until 'al dente'. Drain and toss with the peppers, sauce and butter. Serve immediately.

Broad Beans and Greens

SERVES 4-6

225 g/8 oz shelled young broad beans
800 g/1¾ lb spring greens, kale or Swiss chard
6 tbsp olive oil
1 red onion, finely chopped
3 garlic cloves, finely chopped

3 sage leaves, finely chopped
½ tsp dried chilli flakes
salt and freshly ground black pepper
450 g/1 lb conchiglie, penne or gnocchi
4 tbsp freshly grated Parmesan cheese

*P*LUNGE the broad beans into boiling water for 2 minutes. Drain under cold running water, then slip off the outer skins if they are tough.

❦ Remove the tough stalks from the greens and finely slice the leaves crossways.

❦ Heat the oil in a large pan, and gently fry the onion until just soft. Add the garlic, sage and chilli flakes.

❦ Add the greens and toss the leaves until coated with oil. Cover and cook over a medium heat for 7–10 minutes, until the greens are just tender, adding a little water if the mixture becomes too dry. Stir in the beans and season to taste.

❦ Cook the pasta in boiling salted water until 'al dente'. Drain and toss with the vegetables. Stir in the Parmesan cheese and serve at once.

Roasted Pepper Sauce

SERVES 4-6

6 mixed red and yellow peppers
8 tbsp olive oil
3 garlic cloves, very finely chopped
100 g/4 oz oil-cured black olives, pitted and chopped
4 tbsp finely chopped fresh flat-leafed parsley

½ tsp dried thyme or oregano
½ tsp freshly ground black pepper
450 g/1 lb penne or rigatoni
4 tbsp toasted breadcrumbs
freshly grated Parmesan cheese, to serve

*R*OAST the peppers in a preheated oven at 220°C/425°F/ gas mark 7 for about 5 minutes until the skin blisters and blackens. Allow to cool, then remove the skins and seeds, and slice the flesh into thin strips.

❦ Heat the oil in a large pan and gently fry the garlic until just beginning to colour. Add the peppers, olives, parsley, thyme and black pepper. Stir until heated through.

❦ Cook the pasta in boiling salted water until 'al dente'. Drain and toss with the sauce and breadcrumbs. Serve at once, with Parmesan cheese.

Mushroom and Pine Nut Sauce

SERVES 4

25 g/1 oz dried morels or porcini,
  soaked in 225 ml/8 fl oz warm water
  for 20 minutes
2 tbsp olive oil
25 g/1 oz butter
350 g/12 oz large flat cap mushrooms,
  chopped into 1 cm/½ inch pieces

1 garlic clove, finely chopped
3 tbsp finely chopped fresh parsley
salt and freshly ground black pepper
50 g/2 oz pine nuts, toasted
425 ml/¾ pint double cream
350 g/12 oz fusilli or lumache
4 tbsp freshly grated Parmesan cheese

*D*RAIN the morels, reserving the water, and squeeze to extract excess liquid. Chop into 1 cm/¼ inch pieces.

❧ Strain the soaking water and reserve.

❧ Heat the olive oil and butter in a large pan. Stir-fry the morels and fresh mushrooms over a medium-high heat for 5 minutes.

❧ Stir in the garlic, parsley, and the soaking water. Stir-fry until the liquid has evaporated. Season to taste.

❧ Cook the pasta in boiling salted water until 'al dente'. Drain and toss with the mushrooms. Add the pine nuts, cream and Parmesan cheese. Stir until heated through, and serve at once.

VARIATION: For Mushroom and Asparagus Sauce, use tagliatelle instead of fusilli. Leave out the pine kernels and stir in 175 g/6 oz blanched chopped asparagus with the cream.

Spaghetti Aglio e Olio
(Garlic and Oil Sauce)

SERVES 4-6

125 ml/4 fl oz olive oil
4 garlic cloves, finely chopped
1 fresh red chilli, seeded and finely
  chopped

450 g/1 lb spaghetti
2 tbsp chopped fresh parsley
freshly ground black pepper

*H*EAT the oil in a pan, and fry the garlic and chilli for 1–2 minutes until the garlic is pale golden. Do not allow it to brown.

❧ Cook the spaghetti in boiling salted water until 'al dente'.

❧ Drain and toss with the oil mixture and the parsley. Season with black pepper and serve immediately.

Salsa Primavera
(Spring Vegetable and Cream Sauce)

SERVES 4-6

100 g/4 oz butter
1 onion, diced
1 carrot, diced
1 celery stalk, diced
100 g/4 oz shelled peas
2 ripe tomatoes, peeled and chopped
1 large courgette, cut into 1 cm/
½ inch cubes

100 g/4 oz thin asparagus, stalks
chopped
300 ml/½ pint double cream
salt and freshly ground black pepper
450 g/1 lb fettuccine or tagliatelle
50 g/2 oz freshly grated Parmesan
cheese
2 tbsp finely chopped flat-leafed
parsley

MELT half the butter, and gently fry the onion, carrot and celery until soft. Add the peas, tomatoes and courgette, and gently fry for 5 minutes. Add the asparagus, and fry for 1 minute.

☙ Stir in the cream, and simmer gently until reduced by half. Season to taste.

☙ Cook the pasta in boiling salted water until 'al dente'. Drain and toss with the remaining butter, the Parmesan cheese, parsley and half the sauce. Transfer to a serving dish, spoon the remaining sauce over the top and serve immediately.

Tomato and Garlic Sauce

SERVES 4-6

3 tbsp olive oil
900 g/2 lb plum tomatoes, peeled and
chopped
4 garlic cloves, finely chopped
½ tsp dried oregano

1 tbsp chopped fresh parsley
salt and freshly ground black pepper
450 g/1 lb linguine or spaghetti
freshly grated Parmesan cheese, to
serve

HEAT the oil in a pan, and gently fry the tomatoes and garlic over a medium-high heat for 20 minutes until thickened. Add the oregano, parsley and salt and pepper to taste, and cook for a few minutes more.

☙ Cook the pasta in boiling salted water until 'al dente'. Drain and mix with the sauce. Transfer to a heated dish and serve immediately with the grated Parmesan cheese.

Courgette Sauce with Rosemary

SERVES 4-6

450 g/1 lb courgettes, cut into
   matchstick strips
salt and freshly ground black pepper
5 tbsp olive oil
2 onions, very thinly sliced
1 garlic clove, finely chopped

1 tbsp finely chopped flat-leafed
   parsley
2 tbsp finely chopped fresh rosemary
450 g/1 lb fresh fettuccine
50 g/2 oz freshly grated Parmesan
   cheese

*P*UT the courgettes in a colander, sprinkle with salt and drain for 1 hour. Pat dry with paper towels.

❧ Heat the oil, and gently fry the onion until golden. Add the garlic, parsley and courgettes, and fry until just tender, stirring frequently.

❧ Stir in the rosemary, and season to taste.

❧ Cook the pasta in boiling salted water until 'al dente'. Drain and toss with half the Parmesan cheese and half the sauce. Transfer to a serving dish, and spoon the remaining sauce over the top. Sprinkle with the remaining Parmesan cheese, and serve immediately.

Fresh Tomato Sauce

SERVES 4-6

3 tbsp olive oil
2 celery stalks, finely chopped
1 large carrot, finely chopped
1 small onion, finely chopped
2 garlic cloves, crushed
1 kg/2¼ lb ripe plum tomatoes,
   roughly chopped

1 tsp caster sugar
2 tbsp chopped fresh basil
salt and freshly ground black pepper
450 g/1 lb spaghetti or linguine
torn basil leaves, to garnish
freshly grated Parmesan cheese, to
   serve

*H*EAT the oil, and gently fry the celery, carrot, onion and garlic for 5 minutes until tender.

❧ Stir in the tomatoes, sugar and basil, and season to taste with salt and pepper. Bring to the boil, cover and simmer gently for 30 minutes.

❧ Transfer to a food processor and purée. Rub the purée through a sieve.

❧ Cook the pasta in boiling salted water until 'al dente'. Drain and toss with the sauce. Transfer to a serving dish, garnish with basil, and serve immediately with Parmesan cheese.

Oriental Crabmeat Sauce

SERVES 2-3

2 tbsp groundnut oil
100 g/4 oz drained canned crabmeat
100 g/4 oz spinach or cabbage,
    trimmed and coarsely shredded
1 tsp soy sauce

225 ml/8 fl oz stock
150 g/5 oz egg noodles
salt
1 spring onion, finely chopped, to
    garnish

*H*EAT the oil in a wok until almost smoking, and stir-fry the crabmeat and spinach. Add the soy sauce and stock and stir-fry for 2–3 minutes. Keep warm.

❧ Bring a saucepan of salted water to the boil. Add the noodles and simmer for 5 minutes. Drain and transfer to a warm serving dish.

❧ Pour the sauce over the top and garnish with finely chopped spring onion. Serve immediately.

Prawn, Black Bean and Ginger Sauce

SERVES 4

3 tbsp fermented black beans, rinsed
½ tsp sugar
1 tsp toasted sesame oil
6 tbsp groundnut oil
2.5 cm/1 inch piece fresh ginger root,
    very finely chopped
4 garlic cloves, very finely chopped

1 fresh chilli, seeded and finely
    chopped
450 g/1 lb large peeled prawns
3 tbsp chopped fresh coriander
2 tbsp rice vinegar
350 g/12 oz flat rice noodles, cooked
    as the packet instructions

*M*ASH the beans to a paste with the sugar and sesame oil. Heat 4 tablespoons of the groundnut oil in a wok until almost smoking. Add the ginger, garlic and chilli, and stir-fry for a few seconds.

❧ Add the prawns and coriander, and stir-fry for 3 minutes.

❧ Add the bean paste, then the rice vinegar. Stir well, then remove from the pan and keep warm.

❧ Wipe out the wok and heat the remaining oil. Add the drained noodles and stir over a medium heat until heated through.

❧ Transfer the noodles to a serving dish, top with the prawns and serve immediately.

Black Pasta with Seafood
and Chilli Sauce

SERVES 4

8 tbsp olive oil
1 red pepper, seeded and diced
2 garlic cloves, finely chopped
2 fresh red chillies, seeded and
   chopped
2 tbsp chopped fresh flat-leafed parsley

700 g/1½ lb mixed seafood cocktail
salt and freshly ground black pepper
4 tbsp toasted breadcrumbs
225 g/8 oz black tagliolini or
   spaghetti

*H*EAT the oil in a large pan, and gently fry the pepper until just soft. Add the garlic and chillies, and fry until the garlic starts to change colour.

❧ Add the parsley, then the seafood, and stir-fry for about 5 minutes until heated through. Season to taste.

❧ Cook the pasta in boiling salted water until 'al dente'. Drain and toss with the breadcrumbs and half the sauce. Transfer to a heated serving dish, spoon the remaining sauce over the top, and serve immediately.

Herbed Salmon Sauce

SERVES 4

1 tbsp olive oil
25 g/1 oz butter
350 g/12 oz boned skinned salmon,
   cut into 1 cm/½ inch cubes
4 spring onions, green parts included,
   finely sliced
salt and freshly ground black pepper
50 ml/2 fl oz dry white wine

125 ml/4 fl oz fish stock
500 ml/18 fl oz double cream
3 tbsp finely chopped fresh coriander
1 tbsp each finely chopped fresh
   mint, rocket and lovage
250 g/9 oz spinach fettuccine or
   tagliatelle

*H*EAT the oil and butter in a pan and gently fry the salmon for 3 minutes. Add the onions and fry for 1 minute more. Season to taste. Remove the mixture from the pan with the juices and keep warm.

❧ Add the wine and simmer until reduced by half. Add the fish stock and reduce by half again.

❧ Stir in the cream and herbs, and simmer until thickened and reduced. Gently stir in the salmon, and check the seasoning.

❧ Cook the pasta in boiling salted water until 'al dente'. Drain and toss with the sauce. Serve immediately.

Haddock and Egg Sauce

SERVES 4

450 g/1 lb smoked haddock
350 g/12 oz tagliatelle or fettucine
50 g/2 oz butter
2 tbsp chopped fresh parsley

salt and freshly ground black pepper
3 eggs, beaten
juice of ½ lemon

*P*LACE the fish in a pan, just cover with water and poach for 12–15 minutes or until cooked. Drain, flake the flesh and keep warm.

❧ Cook the pasta in boiling salted water until 'al dente' and drain thoroughly.

❧ Return the pasta to the pan. Add the flaked fish, butter and parsley, and season to taste. Stir in the eggs, and continue stirring until the heat of the pasta cooks the eggs.

❧ Transfer to a serving dish, sprinkle with the lemon juice and serve immediately.

Tuna and Mushroom Sauce

SERVES 4-6

125 ml/4 fl oz olive oil
1 garlic clove, crushed
225 g/8 oz mushrooms, finely sliced
1 small red pepper, seeded and thinly sliced
200 g/7 oz can tuna in oil

salt and freshly ground black pepper
450 g/1 lb penne or macaroni
finely chopped fresh parsley or basil, to garnish

*H*EAT the olive oil in a pan, and gently fry the garlic, mushrooms and pepper for 5 minutes, until the vegetables are tender but still firm.

❧ Flake the tuna but do not drain. Add to the pan and stir gently until the sauce is blended and heated through. Season to taste with salt and pepper.

❧ Cook the pasta in boiling salted water until 'al dente'. Drain and toss with half the sauce.

❧ Transfer to a serving dish and spoon the remaining sauce over the top. Garnish with chopped parsley or basil and serve immediately.

Smoked Salmon and Asparagus Sauce

SERVES 4

350 g/12 oz asparagus
350 g/12 oz tagliatelle or fettuccine
100 g/4 oz smoked salmon, cut into
  thin strips

300 ml/½ pint double cream
1 tbsp chopped fresh tarragon
salt and freshly ground black pepper
Parmesan shavings, to garnish

*C*UT off the asparagus tips and blanch in boiling salted water for 5 minutes. Use the stems for soup or stock. Drain the tips under cold running water, and pat dry.

❧ Cook the pasta in boiling salted water until 'al dente'. Drain and return to the pan. Toss over a low heat with the the asparagus, smoked salmon, cream, tarragon, and salt and pepper, until heated through.

❧ Transfer to a heated serving dish and garnish with wafer-thin shavings of Parmesan cheese.

VARIATION: For Smoked Salmon and Mushroom Sauce, use 350 g/12 oz mixed ceps, shitake, oyster and chestnut mushrooms, instead of the asparagus. Cut into even-sized pieces and stir-fry in 2 tablespoons of olive oil for 5–7 minutes, before adding to the pasta.

Scallop and Fennel Sauce

SERVES 4

8 tbsp olive oil
2 garlic cloves, finely chopped
2 fennel bulbs, trimmed and very
  thinly sliced lengthways
450 g/1 lb scallops, thinly sliced
4 tbsp chopped fresh flat-leafed parsley

salt and freshly ground black pepper
350 g/12 oz fusilli lunghi or linguine
4 tbsp freshly grated Parmesan
  cheese
4 tbsp toasted breadcrumbs

*H*EAT the oil and gently fry the garlic for a few seconds until just pale golden.

❧ Stir in the fennel, cover and cook gently for 5 minutes until just tender.

❧ Add the scallops, parsley, and salt and pepper. Stir-fry over a medium-high heat for 3–5 minutes, then remove from the heat.

❧ Cook the pasta in boiling salted water until 'al dente'. Drain and toss with the sauce, Parmesan cheese and breadcrumbs. Serve at once.

Spaghetti alle Vongole
(Clam and Tomato Sauce)

SERVES 4-6

2 litres/3½ pints fresh clams
150 ml/¼ pint dry white wine
2 tbsp olive oil
3 garlic cloves, finely chopped
700 g/1½ lb tomatoes, peeled and
chopped

2 tbsp chopped fresh flat-leafed
parsley
salt and freshly ground black pepper
450 g/1 lb spaghetti or spaghettini

*S*CRUB the clams under cold running water to remove all sand and grit. Discard any that do not close when tapped. Put the clams in a pan, add the wine, cover and cook for 5 minutes. Strain, reserving the liquid. Remove the clams from the shells. Discard any that have not opened.

❧ Heat the oil in a pan, and gently fry the garlic until just golden. Stir in the tomatoes, and simmer gently for 10 minutes.

❧ Add the clams, the strained cooking liquid and parsley, and season to taste. Heat through for 5 minutes.

❧ Cook the pasta in boiling salted water until 'al dente'. Drain and mix with the sauce over a gentle heat. Transfer to a serving dish and serve immediately.

Prawn Sauce with Sun-Dried Tomatoes
and Mushrooms

SERVES 4

8 tbsp olive oil
350 g/12 oz button mushrooms, sliced
350 g/12 oz large shelled prawns
40 g/1½ oz sun-dried tomatoes,
finely chopped
2 tbsp lemon juice

10 spring onions, sliced
diagonally
3 tbsp chopped fresh basil
salt and freshly ground black pepper
250 g/9 oz spinach spaghetti or
linguine

*H*EAT the oil in a large pan until almost smoking. Add the mushrooms and stir-fry for 2 minutes.

❧ Add the prawns and sun-dried tomatoes, and stir-fry for 3 minutes.

❧ Add the lemon juice and onions, and stir-fry for another 2 minutes. Stir in the basil and season to taste.

❧ Cook the pasta in boiling salted water until 'al dente'. Drain and toss with half the sauce. Transfer to a serving dish, spoon the remaining sauce over the top, and serve immediately.

Mediterranean Fish Sauce

SERVES 6

3 tbsp olive oil
1 small onion, finely chopped
2 garlic cloves, finely chopped
1 small red pepper, seeded and diced
1 small green pepper, seeded and diced
400 g/14 oz can chopped tomatoes

4 tbsp finely chopped flat-leafed
  parsley
450 g/1 lb firm white fish fillets
  e.g. halibut, cod, monkfish, cubed
salt and freshly ground black pepper
450 g/1 lb rigatoni or penne

*H*EAT the oil in a heavy frying pan, and gently fry the onion, garlic and peppers until soft.

❧ Stir in the tomatoes, parsley and fish, and season to taste. Simmer, uncovered, until the fish is just tender.

❧ Cook the pasta in boiling salted water until 'al dente'. Drain and toss with half the sauce. Transfer to a serving dish, spoon the remaining sauce over the top and serve immediately.

Mussels with Saffron Cream Sauce

SERVES 4

large pinch of saffron threads
2 litres/3½ pints mussels, scrubbed
  and bearded
175 ml/6 fl oz dry white wine
2 shallots, finely chopped

150 ml/¼ pint double cream
salt and freshly ground black pepper
225 g/8 oz black tagliolini or
  linguine

*S*OAK the saffron in 2 tablespoons of hot water for about 5 minutes.

❧ Put the mussels in a large pan with the wine and the shallots. Cover and simmer over a high heat for 3 minutes. Remove from the heat and leave to stand for 5 minutes.

❧ Strain the liquid through a coffee filter and pour into a clean pan. Boil until reduced to about 150 ml/¼ pint.

❧ Shell the mussels and keep warm.

❧ Add the cream and the saffron, with its soaking water, to the mussel liquid. Simmer for about 5 minutes until thickened, and season to taste.

❧ Cook the pasta in boiling salted water until 'al dente'. Drain and toss with the mussels. Transfer to a serving dish and pour the sauce over the centre. Serve at once.

Pasta con le Sarde
(Sicilian Sardine Sauce)

SERVES 4

½ tsp saffron threads
1½ tbsp tomato purée
225 ml/8 fl oz hot water
25 g/1 oz raisins
8 tbsp olive oil
½ small onion, finely chopped
1 fennel bulb, finely chopped
1 garlic clove, finely chopped

½ tsp fennel seeds, toasted and crushed
6 anchovy fillets, chopped
450 g/1 lb fresh sardines, filleted
40 g/1½ oz pine nuts, toasted
freshly ground black pepper
350 g/12 oz bucatini or linguine
4 tbsp toasted breadcrumbs

COMBINE the saffron, tomato purée and the hot water, and set aside.

♥ Soak the raisins for 15 minutes in enough hot water to cover, then drain and chop roughly.

♥ Heat the oil in a large pan, and gently fry the onion and fennel until just soft. Add the garlic, fennel seed and anchovies. Fry for a 1–2 minutes, mashing the anchovies to a paste.

♥ Add the sardines and fry briefly on each side.

♥ Stir in the pine nuts, raisins, saffron solution, and pepper. Simmer over a medium heat for 5–7 minutes until the liquid reduces and the sardines break up a little.

♥ Cook the pasta in boiling salted water until 'al dente'. Drain and transfer to a heated serving dish. Toss with the sauce and the breadcrumbs. Serve at once.

Tuna Sauce with Tomatoes and Garlic

SERVES 4-6

2 tbsp olive oil
1 garlic clove, chopped
200 g/7 oz can tuna, drained and coarsely flaked
3 tbsp chopped fresh parsley

2 tbsp tomato purée
225 ml/8 fl oz stock
salt and freshly ground black pepper
450 g/1 lb rigatoni, penne or elbow macaroni

HEAT the oil, and fry the garlic until just beginning to colour. Add the tuna, 2 tablespoons of the parsley, the tomato purée and stock. Season to taste with salt and pepper. Simmer gently for 15 minutes.

♥ Cook the pasta in boiling salted water until 'al dente'. Drain, mix with the tuna sauce and transfer to a serving dish.

♥ Sprinkle with the remaining chopped parsley and serve immediately.

Mixed Seafood Sauce

SERVES 4-6

50 g/2 oz butter or margarine
1 onion, finely chopped
1 garlic clove, crushed
50 g/2 oz flour
450 ml/¾ pint vegetable stock
150 ml/¼ pint white wine
100 g/4 oz monkfish, cubed
6 scallops, cut into quarters

50 g/2 oz canned or frozen crabmeat, thawed
100 g/4 oz peeled prawns
1 tbsp chopped fresh marjoram
salt and freshly ground black pepper
150 ml/¼ pint single cream
450 g/1 lb conchiglie or orecchiette

*M*ELT the butter in a saucepan, and gently fry the onion and garlic for 2 minutes.

❦ Stir in the flour and cook for 1 minute. Gradually add the stock and wine, stirring continuously. Bring to the boil.

❦ Reduce the heat and stir in the monkfish and scallops. Cook gently for 2–3 minutes.

❦ Stir in the crabmeat, prawns and marjoram, season with salt and pepper, and heat gently for 1 minute.

❦ Add the cream and heat through.

❦ Cook the pasta in boiling salted water until 'al dente'. Drain and toss with half the sauce. Transfer to a serving dish, spoon the remaining sauce over the top and serve immediately.

Chillied Prawn Sauce

SERVES 4

3 onions, chopped
2 garlic cloves, finely chopped
25 g/1 oz mixed nuts, chopped
2 tsp salt
½ tsp chilli powder
¼ tsp powdered saffron
½ tsp grated lemon zest

2 tsp anchovy paste
3 tbsp vegetable oil
700 g/1½ lb peeled prawns
75 g/3 oz finely shredded coconut
425 ml/¾ pint milk
225 g/8 oz vermicelli or spaghettini

*P*UT the onions, garlic, nuts, salt, chilli, saffron, lemon zest and anchovy paste in a blender and purée until smooth.

❦ Heat the oil in a frying pan, and gently fry the mixture for 3 minutes, stirring constantly. Stir in the prawns, and fry for 2 minutes. Add the coconut and milk, bring to the boil and cook over a low heat for 1 minute.

❦ Cook the pasta in boiling salted water until 'al dente'. Drain and toss with half the sauce. Transfer to a serving dish, spoon the remaining sauce over the top and serve immediately.

A

Aubergine, Pepper and Olive Sauce 30
Aubergine, Tomato and Chilli Sauce 36
Avocado and Cream Sauce 26

B

Bacon and Broad Bean Sauce 24
Bacon and Egg Sauce see Spaghetti alla Carbonara
Bacon, Mushroom and Tomato Sauce 22
Black Pasta with Seafood and Chilli Sauce 50
Bolognese Sauce 6
Broad Beans and Greens 40
Broccoli Sauce with Chilli 38

C

Chick-Pea and Tomato Sauce 28
Chicken and Tomato Sauce 10
Chicken Liver Sauce 12
Chillied Prawn Sauce 62
Chinese Chicken and Mushroom Sauce 10
Clam and Tomato Sauce see Spaghetti alle Vongole
Conchiglie with Peperoni, Onion and Balsamic Vinegar 24
Courgette Sauce with Rosemary 46
Cream Cheese and Walnut Sauce 34

F

Farfalle with Herbed Savoy Cabbage 36
Fresh Herb and Lemon Sauce 30
Fresh Tomato Sauce 46

G

Garlic and Oil Sauce see Spaghetti Aglio e Olio

H

Haddock and Egg Sauce 52
Ham and Mushroom Sauce 8
Ham, Pea and Mushroom Sauce 20
Ham, Tomato and Cheese Sauce 14
Herbed Salmon Sauce 50

L

Leek and Green Peppercorn Sauce 32

M

Mediterranean Fish Sauce 58
Mixed Seafood Sauce 62
Mushroom and Asparagus Sauce 42
Mushroom and Pine Nut Sauce 42
Mussels with Saffron Cream Sauce 58

O

Oriental Crabmeat Sauce 48

P

Pancetta and Celery Sauce 18
Pancetta with Flageolet Beans, Garlic and Chilli 16
Pasta con le Sarde 60
Pesto Sauce 32
Pork and Rosemary Sauce 16
Pork Chow Mein 12
Prawn Sauce with Sun-Dried Tomatoes and Mushrooms 56
Prawn, Black Bean and Ginger Sauce 48

Prosciutto and Pea Sauce 6
Prosciutto, Chilli and Tomato Sauce 22

R

Rabbit and Red Wine Sauce 18
Raw Tomato Sauce with Basil 26
Roasted Pepper Sauce 40
Roasted Peppers with Coriander and Chilli Pesto 38
Rocket, Garlic and Chilli Sauce 28

S

Salsa Primavera 44
Sausage and Tomato Sauce 8
Scallop and Fennel Sauce 54
Sicilian Sardine Sauce see Pasta con le Sarde
Smoked Salmon and Asparagus Sauce 54
Smoked Salmon and Mushroom Sauce 54
Spaghetti Aglio e Olio 42
Spaghetti alla Carbonara 20
Spaghetti alle Vongole 56
Spinach Tagliatelle with Bacon and Fennel 14
Spring Vegetable and Cream Sauce see Salsa Primavera

T

Tomato and Garlic Sauce 44
Tomato, Anchovy and Olive Sauce 34
Tuna and Mushroom Sauce 52
Tuna Sauce with Tomatoes and Garlic 60
Types of Pasta 4